A Note to Parents and Caregivers:

Read-it! Joke Books are for children who are moving ahead on the amazing road to reading. These fun books support the acquisition and extension of reading skills as well as a love of books.

Published by the same company that produces *Read-it!* Readers, these books introduce the question/answer and dialogue patterns that help children expand their thinking about language structure and book formats.

When sharing joke books with a child, read in short stretches. Pause often to talk about the meaning of the jokes. The question/answer and dialogue formats work well for this purpose and provide an opportunity to talk about the language and meaning of the jokes. Have the child turn the pages and point to the pictures and familiar words. When you read the jokes, have fun creating the voices of characters or emphasizing some important words. Be sure to reread favorite jokes.

There is no right or wrong way to share books with children. Find time to read with your child, and pass on the legacy of literacy.

Adria F. Klein, Ph.D.
Professor Emeritus
California State University
San Bernardino, California

Editor: Jill Kalz
Designer: Joe Anderson
Page Production: Melissa Kes
Creative Director: Keith Griffin
Editorial Director: Carol Jones
The illustrations in this book were created digitally.

Picture Window Books
5115 Excelsior Boulevard
Suite 232
Minneapolis, MN 55416
877-845-8392
www.picturewindowbooks.com

Printed in the United States of America.

Library of Congress Cataloging-in-Publication Data
Donahue, Jill L.
Family follies : a book of family jokes / by Jill L. Donahue ; illustrated by
Zachary Trover.
p. cm. – (Read-it! joke books–supercharged!)
Includes bibliographical references.
ISBN-13: 978-1-4048-2362-4 (hardcover)
ISBN-10: 1-4048-2362-X (hardcover)
1. Family–Juvenile humor. 2. Riddles, Juvenile. I. Trover, Zachary. II. Title. III. Series.
PN6231.F3D66 2006
818'.602–dc22   2006003562

FAMILY FOLLIES

A Book of Family Jokes

by Jill L. Donahue
illustrated by Zachary Trover

Special thanks to our advisers for their expertise:

Adria F. Klein, Ph.D.
Professor Emeritus, California State University
San Bernardino, California

Susan Kesselring, M.A.
Literacy Educator
Rosemount–Apple Valley–Eagan (Minnesota) School District

PiCTURE WiNDOW BOOKS
Minneapolis, Minnesota

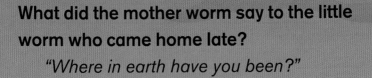

What did the mother worm say to the little worm who came home late?

"Where in earth have you been?"

Mom: "Bobby, there were two pieces of cake on the counter last night, and now there is only one. Can you explain?"

Bobby: "Sure. It was dark in the kitchen, and I didn't see the other piece sitting there!"

Where did the ghost's baby brother go during the day?

To day scare.

Where did the family take their crying children?

To the "ballpark."

Dad: "Don't you think our daughter gets all of her brains from me?"

Mom: "Probably. I still have all of mine."

What did the father firefly say to his son?

"For a little guy, you're very bright."

Why couldn't the boy read his sister a story about a bed?

It hadn't been made up yet.

Son: "Mom, do you want to play hide-and-seek?"

Mom: "Sure, I even have a special tool that will help me find you quickly!"

Son: "What's that?"

Mom: "My 'sunglasses.'"

Why did Dad put a clock under his desk at work?

He wanted to work overtime.

Why are monster children usually very good children?

Because they respect their mummies.

Mom: "What did you learn in school today?"
"... apparently not enough. I have to go
... morrow."

Amanda: "Where does your sister live?"
Ashley: "Alaska."
Amanda: "Never mind, I'll ask her myself if you don't know."

Why did the nasty boy put ice cubes in his aunt's bed?

Because he wanted to make auntifreeze.

Why did the bald father paint rabbits on his head?

He wanted some "hares" on his head.

When do monster mothers receive gifts?
On Mummy's Day.

Dad: "What do you want for your birthday, Son?"
Son: "Nothing much really—just a new radio with a sports car wrapped around it."

Why did the little boy eat the change?

His mom told him it was his lunch money.

What kind of sisters do robots have?

Transisters.

What kind of keys do kids like to eat?
Cookies.

What did the mother hamburger name her daughter?
Patty.

What did the little lightbulb say to his mom?
"I love you watts and watts."

What did the baby rabbit want to do when she grew up?
Join the Hare Force.

Billy: "Mom, have you noticed that Dad is getting taller?"

Mom: "No, why?"

Billy: "His head is starting to stick through his hair."

Where do fish families go on vacation?

To Finland.

Welcome to FINLAND

DAUGH
UNCLE
GRANDPA
MOTHER
SON
BROTH
SISTE
MOTHER
SON
ON

What did the mother broom say to her baby?

"It's time to go to sweep."

Who was bigger, Mr. Bigger or his son?

The son was a little Bigger.

What did the baby ghost want to do when he grew up?

Join the Ghost Guard.

Mom: "How was your report card?"

Son: "My marks are all underwater."

Mom: "What does that mean?"

Son: "They are all below C-level."

Why was the shoe unhappy?
Because his father was a loafer,
and his mother was a sneaker.

Why did the little sister take her bike to bed?
She didn't want to walk in her sleep.

Big brother: "That planet up there is Mars."
Little sister: "Then that other planet must be Pa's."

Boy: "Why did your sister refuse the door prize she just won?"
Girl: "She already has a door."

Abby: "Why does your sister keep running around her bed?"

Gabby: "She says she's trying to catch up on her sleep."

Why did the boy ask his dad to sit inside the freezer?

He wanted an ice-cold pop.

Daughter: "Dad, there's a man at the door collecting for the new city pool."
Dad: "Well, don't just stand there. Give him a glass of water."

Why did the big sister go to night school?
She wanted to learn to read in the dark.

What do you call a mom who is very small?
Minimum.

What do you call a carpenter's son?

A chip off the old block.

Why did the man who had two sons name them both Ed?

Because two Eds are better than one.

Teacher: "Class, where did the Pilgrims come from?"
Students: "Their parents, of course!"

Son: "Dad, the dentist wasn't painless like you said he would be."
Dad: "Really? Did he hurt you?"
Son: "No, but he did yell in pain when I bit his finger."

Friend: "Does your dad always snore?"
Boy: "No, only when he is asleep."

What did the daddy ghost say to the young ghost who wouldn't stop talking?
"Spook when you are spoken to!"

Mom: "Why do you always get so dirty?"
Son: "I'm a lot closer to the ground than you are."

Why did Mom go to bed with a ruler?

To see how long she could sleep.

How did Dad feel when he got the big bill from the electric company?

He was shocked.

Read-it! Joke Books— Supercharged!

Chitchat Chuckles: A Book of Funny Talk 1-4048-1160-5

Creepy Crawlers: A Book of Bug Jokes 1-4048-0627-X

Fur, Feathers, and Fun! A Book of Animal Jokes 1-4048-1161-3

Lunchbox Laughs: A Book of Food Jokes 1-4048-0963-5

Mind Knots: A Book of Riddles 1-4048-1162-1

Nutty Names: A Book of Name Jokes 1-4048-1163-X

Roaring with Laughter: A Book of Animal Jokes 1-4048-0628-8

Sit! Stay! Laugh! A Book of Pet Jokes 1-4048-0629-6

Wacky Workers: A Book of Job Jokes 1-4048-1164-8

What's Up, Doc? A Book of Doctor Jokes 1-4048-1165-6

Artful Antics: A Book of Art, Music, and Theater Jokes
   1-4048-2363-8

Laughing Letters and Nutty Numerals: A Book of Jokes About
   ABCs and 123s 1-4048-2365-4

What's in a Name? A Book of Name Jokes 1-4048-2364-6

Looking for a specific title or level? A complete list
of *Read-it!* Readers is available on our Web site:
www.picturewindowbooks.com